BIBLE
BIRDS AND BEASTIES

Leena Lane and T. S. Spookytooth

Contents

Creatures great and small 6

Lots of birds and beasties 8

A raven, a dove and a rainbow 10

The patient camels 12

Beasties in Egypt 14

The donkey who saw an angel 16

Balaam's talking donkey 18

The donkeys that wandered 20

The helpful ravens 22

A big fish and a stormy sea 24

The fish that swallowed a man 26

The tight-mouthed lions 28

A baby in the cattle shed 30

The sheep who heard angels 32

The camels who followed a star 34

Camels, gifts and a king 36

The little sparrows 38

The very special sheep 40

A lost sheep is found 42

The donkey who carried a king 44

Bible index 46

Creatures great and small

In the beginning, God made the whole world.
God made light to shine in the darkness, dry ground in the middle of salty seas and planets and stars, sun and moon, day and night.

And God made creatures in the sea, land and sky: scaly fish and snapping crocodiles; feathered flamingos and proud peacocks; leaping lizards, terrifying tigers and raging rhinos; calm cows, plump pigs and creepy crawlies; chattering chimps, silent sloths, zigzag zebra and long-necked giraffes.

Many shapes and different sizes, funny smells and snorty noises—
God made creatures, great and small.

But God wanted a creature who would share his likeness, a
creature who could love and be loved, think and feel and create;
a creature who was capable of caring about other creatures and
looking after his world. So God made man and woman.

God saw all that he had made, and it was very good.

Lots of birds and beasties

God had told Noah it was going to rain very, very hard. Soon there would be a great flood. Everything would be washed away—except Noah, his family and all kinds of birds and beasties.

God told Noah to build an ark (a huge boat) and to fill it with lots of food. Then Noah should wait for the rain to come.

When the ark was ready, the animals came down from the trees. They padded, plodded and galloped, hopped, jumped, scampered, slithered and crawled in through the door.

Two by two, male and female, the animals were crowded into the ark. It was hot. It was noisy. It was SMELLY!

Noah and his family climbed aboard and BANG! The door was shut.

A raven, a dove and a rainbow

Splish, splash, splish, splash, the rain began to fall.

Steadily, heavily, the rain fell on the streams till they became rivers, the rivers became seas and the seas covered the earth and the trees and the mountains… until there was nothing left to see, except the ark, floating on the waters.

One day the rain stopped. Noah and his family and the animals listened. There was nothing. No sound at all.

Then days and weeks and months passed. Slowly, slowly the flood waters went down. The sun came out and slowly, slowly the land dried up.

Noah set free a raven and then a dove. Noah set free a second dove until… flap, flap, coo, coo, it returned carrying an olive leaf.

Finally, God told Noah it was safe for his family and all the animals to come out of the ark.

The animals hooted and tooted, roared and bleated and trumpeted as they spread out from the ark on to the new, clean earth.

Then God sent a beautiful rainbow.

'There will never be a flood like this again,' God promised.

Noah thanked God for keeping them safe from the flood, for giving them a chance to start all over again.

The patient camels

The camels spat as the dust swirled up all around them.

It was time to set off again across the rough, stony ground.
Off to Egypt…

Joseph's hands were tied together and fastened to a rope.
All he could see in front of him as he stumbled through the sand
were the backs of the patient camels.

'Where are we going?' he cried desperately. No reply; only the
soft padding of the camels' hooves.

Joseph knew he was in big trouble.

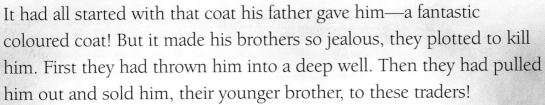

It had all started with that coat his father gave him—a fantastic coloured coat! But it made his brothers so jealous, they plotted to kill him. First they had thrown him into a deep well. Then they had pulled him out and sold him, their younger brother, to these traders!

God had great plans for Joseph in Egypt. Joseph became second only to the great king in wealth and power—and later, he was able to save his whole family from starvation in a famine.

But this was a future he could not even imagine, as Joseph stumbled in the sand behind the patient, plodding camels.

Beasties in Egypt

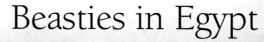

Moses, and all God's people, had been made slaves by the cruel king of Egypt. Now Moses stood in front of the great man himself, with a message that sounded so bold it was frightening.

'God says that you must set his people free, or there will be trouble you cannot even imagine.'

The king would not listen. So God sent terrible plagues on the land of Egypt.

The river turned to blood. The land teemed with thousands of frogs that found their way into beds and cooking pots! There were plagues of biting gnats and buzzing flies. Then the cows, sheep, goats and horses fell ill and died. There were boils upon the skin

of all the Egyptians and hail fell upon the land, damaging the barley and wheat crops. A plague of locusts came to eat up anything left after the hailstorm. Darkness covered the land. And then, the most terrible plague of all—all the Egyptian firstborn sons died in a single night, including Pharaoh's own son.

'God says, "Let my people go!"' said Moses.

'Yes!' said Pharaoh in despair. 'Go!'

Moses did not wait for Pharaoh to change his mind! He led God's people out of Egypt, the land where they had been slaves.

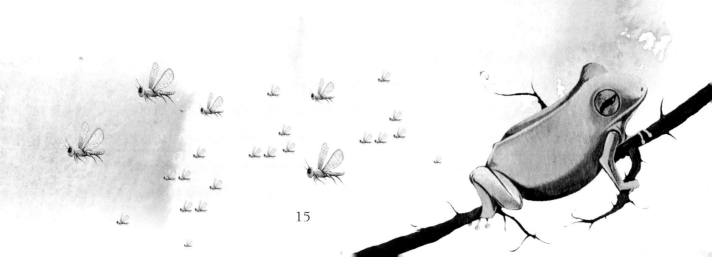

The donkey who saw an angel

Balaam thought he was wiser than God. He set off on a journey one day with his donkey—even though God had told him not to go!

As they started out, an angel appeared holding a sword and blocking their path. The donkey saw the angel and turned off the road into a field. But Balaam was not as wise as the donkey. He saw nothing. He beat the poor old donkey with a stick. Ouch!

The donkey got back on to the road. But now the angel was standing in a narrow path between two walls. The donkey jumped to one side and squashed Balaam's leg against the wall.

Balaam still saw nothing! He couldn't understand why the donkey was being so awkward. He beat her again with his stick. Ouch!

The angel moved on ahead of them to a place where there was no room to turn around. The donkey could do nothing else but stop and lie down on the ground.

Balaam's talking donkey

Balaam beat his donkey with his stick. He was very angry.

But since Balaam was not wise enough to see the angel, God let the donkey speak to him.

'What have I done to you? Why have you hit me three times with your stick?' cried the donkey.

Balaam was astounded. 'You've made me look stupid!' he answered.

'But I'm your dear old donkey!' said the donkey. 'I have never disobeyed you before. Surely you knew I wouldn't do it now without good reason!'

Then Balaam saw the angel too.

'Why have you beaten your donkey three times?' asked the angel. 'She saved your life by turning away and not trying to pass me.'

'I was stubborn,' Balaam answered. 'I should have listened to God, and done only what he told me. I am sorry! I will do whatever he asks.'

The donkey never spoke again, but Balaam was careful to listen… to God!

The donkeys that wandered

God's people wanted to choose a king so they could be like all the other countries around them. Who should it be?

God told the prophet, Samuel, that it would be Saul, who would come to him, looking for his father's lost donkeys.

Saul was a tall, handsome young man. When the donkeys wandered off, Saul took a servant and looked everywhere for them.

'We could ask Samuel, the man of God,' said the servant. 'If anyone knows, he will.'

When Samuel saw Saul coming towards him, God told him that this was the man who would be king.

'Don't worry about your lost donkeys,' said Samuel to Saul straight away. 'I know what you are looking for, and they are safe—but come with me. I am looking for you!'

After they had eaten together, Samuel poured some oil over

Saul's head. 'God has a very special job for you to do,' he said, 'and God will help you do it well.'

Saul found the wandering donkeys— and he found much more at the same time. Now he knew what God wanted him to do with his life. He would be the first king of Israel.

21

The helpful ravens

Elijah had made himself very unpopular with the wicked King Ahab.

He had given the king a very special message from God—Ahab must stop worshipping statues made of wood and stone, or God would not send rain to the earth. Ahab was so angry that Elijah had to run away, fearing for his life!

No rain fell on the earth. Weeks passed and the earth became dry and cracked. The rivers dried up. But Elijah knew that God would look after him.

God told Elijah where to go to hide from the king.

'Drink from the water of this stream,' said God, 'and I will send ravens with food for you to eat.'

God kept his promise. When Elijah was thirsty, he drank the clear water from the stream. When he was hungry, he waited for the ravens to come. There would be a flapping of black

wings and the large birds appeared. Every morning and evening
they brought meat and bread to Elijah. God gave him everything he
needed.

The ravens kept coming until it was time to move on.

A big fish and a stormy sea

Jonah was sinking deep into salty sea water in the middle of a great storm. He was sure he would drown. And he knew it was all his fault.

Jonah had tried to run away from God. He was supposed to go to the great city of Nineveh to tell the people to stop doing bad things. He was supposed to tell them that God could forgive them if they would change their ways—but Jonah didn't want to do it. Why should God forgive the wicked people who lived there? They deserved their punishment!

So Jonah had jumped aboard a ship going the other way. But when a terrible storm had blown up, Jonah knew God had caused it to stop him running away. He told the sailors to throw him over the side into the choppy waves.

The fish that swallowed a man

Now all Jonah could do was pray. He called out to God—and God saved him.

God sent a huge fish to swallow him whole. He opened its mouth and Jonah washed inside. Jonah lived in the body of the fish for three days. It was very dark and smelt very fishy. But Jonah had time to think and to pray.

He was sorry he hadn't done what God had asked him. He knew what he had to do.

The big fish spat Jonah out on to the beach.

The next time God spoke, Jonah listened. He went to the people of Nineveh and gave them God's message. And the people listened too. They stopped doing wicked things and asked God to forgive them. And because God loved them, he did.

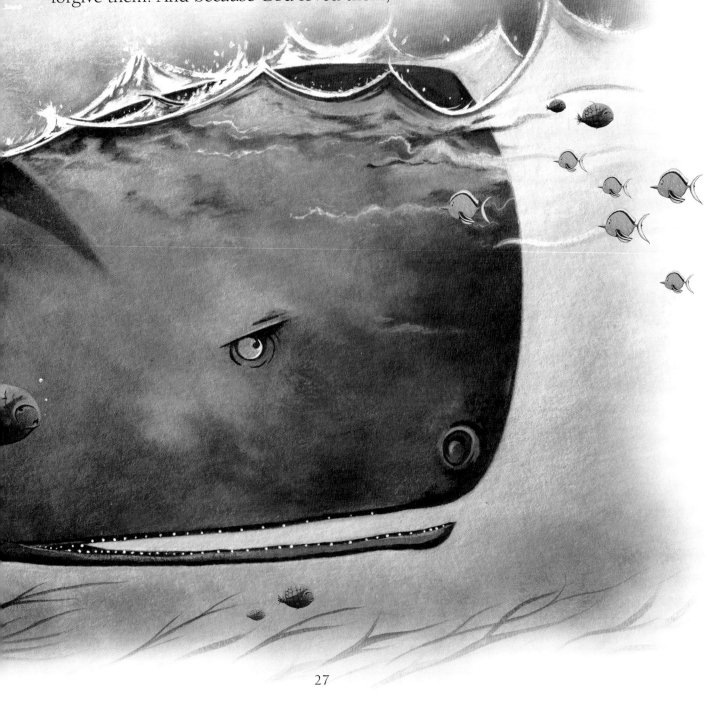

The tight-mouthed lions

Daniel loved God. So when the order came in Babylon that no one should pray to anyone except the king, Daniel could not obey it. He prayed to God alone, just as he did every day.

It was no surprise when Daniel was bound and dragged away to be thrown into the den of hungry lions. He had broken the law of the land.

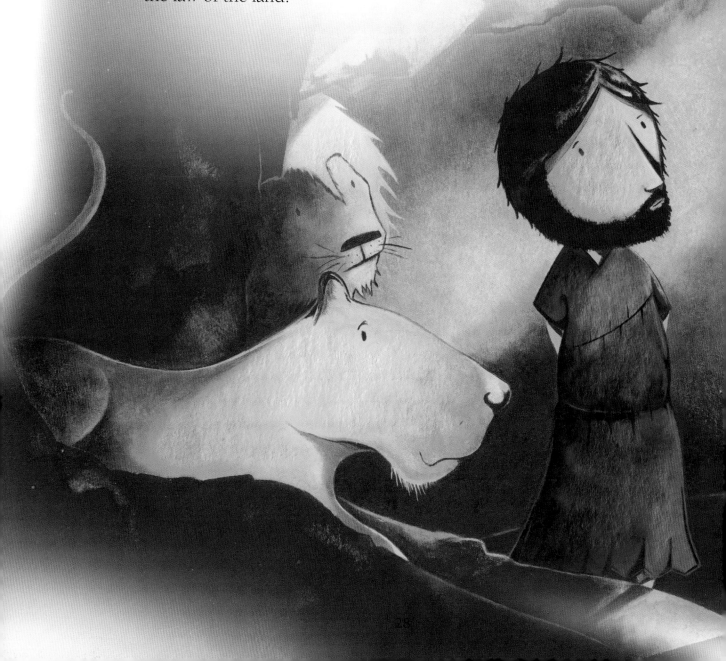

But the lions went hungry that night. God sent an angel to close their mouths so that Daniel, God's faithful servant, would be safe.

Night came and went. The king, who had been tricked into passing the law by Daniel's enemies, hurried to the den at first light.

'Daniel! Daniel! Has your God saved you?' the king shouted.

'Yes!' called out the man among the lions. 'God saved me from the lions. God knew that I loved him and had done nothing wrong.'

The king was overjoyed. He commanded soldiers to release Daniel.

'Now everyone in the land will worship the God of Daniel,' said the king, 'for he has the power to rescue, even from the mouths of lions.'

A baby in the cattle shed

Outside was the sound of the cicadas. Inside the calves were snuffling in the straw and the ox and donkey were munching on the hay.

Mary tried to rest. This was not how she had imagined it, the birth of her firstborn child. She thought she would be at home, with her mother and neighbours to help her. She thought she would be lying on her own bed in Nazareth. But she was here in Bethlehem, surrounded by animals and with no one but Joseph to help.

Then Mary remembered the words of
the angel Gabriel, who had told her
she would be the mother of God's
own son: 'Do not be afraid, Mary…'
The cry of an infant broke the
stillness of the night and Mary
cradled her new baby in her arms.

'Hello, baby Jesus,' she
whispered. She wrapped her little
boy in clean cloths and held him
close. Then she put him in the
manger to sleep, with the ox and
donkey looking on.

The sheep who heard angels

The sheep were sleeping on the hills near Bethlehem.

Some were cuddled together, some were still bleating as they tried to get comfortable for the night.

Then suddenly, the sky was filled with dazzling light! The sheep started awake and stared with the shepherds at the sight of first one, then many angels, filling the sky.

'Don't be afraid!' the angel said. 'I have come to bring good news! A baby has been born today who is the Saviour of the world, Christ the Lord. Go to Bethlehem where you will find him wrapped in cloths and lying in a manger.'

What could this mean? Angels, here, visiting ordinary shepherds with their sheep?

Then the sound of angel song filled the air:

'Praise God in heaven! Peace on earth to everyone who pleases God.'

There had never been such a wonderful sight; there had never been such a beautiful sound. It was the music of heaven.

Then the shepherds left their sheep—
and went to find the special baby.

The camels who followed a star

The camels knelt as their masters threw over brightly coloured tasselled rugs. They secured their packs and mounted their saddles. The camels struggled to their feet and turned their heads to the tug of their harnesses.

The dark night was still studded with stars. One seemed brighter, larger, shining out, a jewel among all the others, and the camels saw that this star was always before them on the journey. The camels and their masters seemed to be following the bright star.

'A new star,' mused one of the men, seated high on the camel's back. 'A sign in the heavens; the birth of a child born to be king.'

'How long do you think we'll be on the road?' called another, bumping rhythmically in his saddle.

'Some long time,' said
the other. 'But we'll find
him. The star will
guide us to the
right place.'

Camels, gifts and a king

The camels were pleased to stop in Jerusalem.

The streets were narrow here, the houses packed tightly together, but the palace had water, even for camels.

The rest was briefer than they had expected. The king here did not look happy, but he was waving them off as they turned from the cobbled streets and back on to sandy ground, the star still shining in front of them.

The house where they stopped was on hilly ground but there was a warm light inside. A woman stood with a young child in her arms.

'We have come to worship the new king!' said one of the men. 'We have travelled from the east.'

The men opened their packs and presented the beautiful gifts they had brought with them: gold, frankincense and myrrh; gifts for a king. Then they bowed low to worship her son, the child whose name was Jesus, before returning home.

Mary treasured their gifts, but she sat thoughtfully for some time afterwards, wondering at these men who had travelled so far.

The little sparrows

There were many amazing creatures among those God made.

Some were long-necked and some had funny tails. Some had pretty feathers and some had scaly skins. Some had striped coats and some had patterns.

Sparrows fluttered about in their hundreds. The little brown birds were not the largest or the most beautiful of God's creatures. But God loved each one of them.

When Jesus grew up, he told people many things about God. He told them that loving God and following his ways would be the best thing they ever did. But it would not always be easy.

Jesus told them that not everyone would be kind to them. Sometimes the right thing would be difficult. But Jesus told them not to be afraid. He looked at the little brown birds hopping around them.

'Two sparrows are sold for a penny,' said Jesus. 'But God feeds them and looks after them. He knows when they fly from their nests and he knows when they fall. If he cares about the sparrows, he cares even more about you! He knows even how many hairs are on your head. So don't be afraid. God will take care of you.'

39

The very special sheep

Jesus often told stories to explain what God was like.

Once he told a story about a shepherd who owned a hundred sheep.

The sheep were all shapes and sizes, young and old, fat and scrawny. But they had one thing in common. They were all special to him.

The shepherd loved each one of them and cared for them, night and day. He made sure they had food and water, and he protected them from danger.

Wolves and bears crept about at night,
trying to snatch the lambs away from
the flock. But the shepherd had a strong
stick to protect his sheep. He didn't
want even one of them to be taken by
wild animals or thieves.

A lost sheep is found

One day, the shepherd counted his sheep and noticed that he had only 99: one was missing.

The shepherd set off to find his lost sheep. He looked over the high ground, in the valleys, behind rocks, inside caves. The shepherd called out in a loud voice.

Then he heard a faint bleating sound. The sheep had heard his voice and recognised him.

The shepherd untangled him from the brambles, lifted him up on to his shoulders and carried him home.

'Look!' he called to his friends. 'I've found my lost sheep! What a happy day it is for me!'

Jesus is sometimes called the Good Shepherd. He cares about all of his followers, just like the shepherd in the story cared for his sheep.

The donkey who carried a king

Princes and kings choose the finest horses to ride. They sit high up in the saddle and everyone knows that they are important. Even *they* think they are important.

But when Jesus rode into Jerusalem, he didn't choose a fine horse. Jesus chose a donkey, a gentle, ordinary donkey.

The young donkey was standing with its mother when two men came and untied them. They placed blankets over the young donkey's back and helped Jesus climb on.

Jesus had healed people who were ill and been kind to the poor. Blind people could see, deaf people could hear and lame people could walk because of Jesus. Most important of all, Jesus had told them how much God loved them.

So as Jesus rode towards the city gates, a large crowd gathered. Soon the donkey was walking over people's soft cloaks instead of stony ground. Then he felt cool palms under his hooves as people cut branches from the trees and laid them down. All around them, people were shouting and cheering, 'Hosanna! Hosanna!'

The young donkey carried Jesus into the great city of Jerusalem. Jesus, the king, had come.

Bible stories can be found as follows:

Creatures great and small, Genesis 1:1–31
Lots of birds and beasties, Genesis 6:8—7:16
A raven, a dove and a rainbow, Genesis 7:17—8:22, 9:8–17
The patient camels, Genesis 37:3–28
Beasties in Egypt, Exodus 3:7–10, 7:14—12:32
The donkey who saw an angel, Numbers 22:21–27
Balaam's talking donkey, Numbers 22:28–34
The donkeys that wandered, 1 Samuel 9:1—10:1
The helpful ravens, 1 Kings 17:1—6
A big fish and a stormy sea, Jonah 1:1–16
The fish that swallowed a man, Jonah 1:17—3:10
The tight-mouthed lions, Daniel 6:1–27
A baby in the cattle shed, Luke 2:4–7
The sheep who heard angels, Luke 2:8–16
The camels who followed a star, Matthew 2:1–2
Camels, gifts and a king, Matthew 2:3–11
The little sparrows, Matthew 10:29–31
The very special sheep, Luke 15:3–4; John 10:14–16
A lost sheep is found, Luke 15:5–7; John 10:14
The donkey who carried a king, Luke 19:29–38